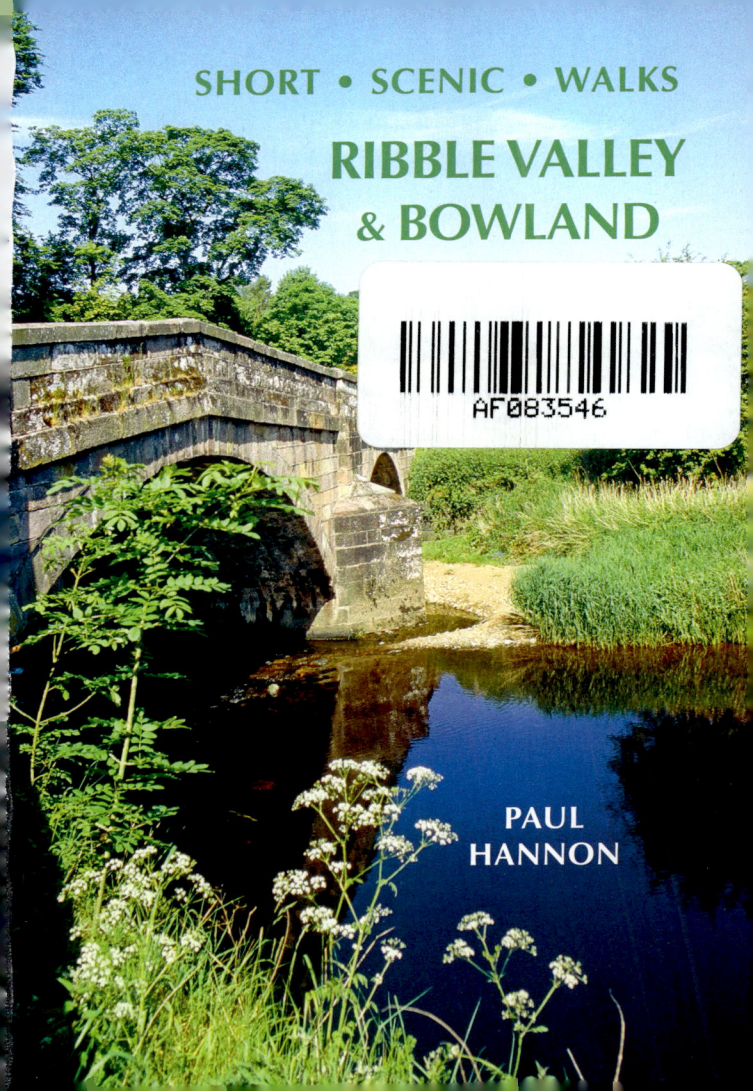

SHORT • SCENIC • WALKS

RIBBLE VALLEY & BOWLAND

PAUL HANNON

HILLSIDE PUBLICATIONS
2 New School Lane, Cullingworth, Bradford BD13 5DA

First Published 2021   © Paul Hannon 2021

ISBN 978 1 907626 38 8

While the author has walked and researched all these routes for the purposes of this guide, no responsibility can be accepted for any unforeseen circumstances encountered whilst following them

Sketch maps based on OS 1947 1-inch maps

Cover illustrations: Langden Brook; Newton-in-Bowland
Back cover: Ribble, Waddington; Page 1: Hodder, Newton Bridge
(Paul Hannon/Yorkshire Photo Library)

Printed in China on behalf of Latitude Press

HILLSIDE GUIDES... cover much of Northern England

- 50 Yorkshire Walks For All   • Journey of the Wharfe (photobook)

Short Scenic Walks •Ribble Valley & Bowland •Wharfedale & Ilkley
- Three Peaks & Malham • North York Moors • Teesdale & Weardale
- Harrogate & Nidderdale • Wensleydale & Swaledale
- Ambleside & South Lakeland • Arnside & Lunesdale
- Aire Valley   • Haworth   • Hebden Bridge   • Around Pendle

Walking in Yorkshire
- North York Moors South & West
- Nidderdale & Ripon
- Wharfedale & Malham
- Aire Valley & Bronte Country
- Yorkshire Wolds
- South Yorkshire
- Three Peaks & Howgill Fells
- North York Moors North & East
- Wensleydale & Swaledale
- Harrogate & Ilkley
- Howardian Hills & Vale of York
- Calderdale & South Pennines
- West Yorkshire Countryside

Lancashire/Cumbria
- Pendle & the Ribble   • Eden Valley

Visit us at www.hillsidepublications.co.uk

CONTENTS

Introduction..........................4

1. Bolton Park.....................6
2. Around Sawley...............8
3. Twiston Beck.................10
4. Pendle Hill.....................12
5. Downham Landscapes...14
6. West Bradford Fell.........16
7. Easington Fell................18
8. Ribble at Waddington....20
9. Great Mitton.................22
10. Nick of Pendle..............24
11. Deerstones....................26
12. Whalley Banks..............28
13. Ribble Woodlands........30
14. Ribchester Dewponds....32
15. Under Longridge............34
16. Stonyhurst College........36
17. Three Rivers..................38
18. Hodder Bridges.............40
19. Longridge Fell..............42
20. River Brock..................44
21. Parlick..........................46
22. Chipping Landscapes....48
23. Around Whitewell........50
24. Little Bowland..............52
25. Hodder Bank Fell..........54
26. Newton-in-Bowland.....56
27. River Hodder................58
28. Croasdale.....................60
29. Trough of Bowland........62
30. Langden Valley.............64

Downham

Langden Valley

INTRODUCTION

The Forest of Bowland Area of Outstanding Natural Beauty is at the heart of rural North Lancashire. Its great dome of rolling moorland falls first to the softer country of the sparkling River Hodder, which then leads into the Ribble Valley overlooked by the brooding mass of Pendle Hill. Further colourful pockets of open country are found on Longridge Fell and Waddington Fell, while both the Ribble and the Hodder offer delectable sections of river-bank walking, never far from delightful villages such as Slaidburn, Newton, Downham and Hurst Green.

Having made a major contribution to the Yorkshire Dales landscape, the Ribble moves on to become Lancashire's finest river on its way to the sea beyond Preston. Midway along its course and very much the focal point of this region is Clitheroe, a bustling market town watched over by a Norman keep sat on its limestone knoll. History abounds too at Sawley, Whalley and Ribchester, while many fine old houses with mullioned windows and weathered datestones reach back through the centuries. Today the Ribble Valley's string of villages is firmly on the visitor's trail, and the likes of Waddington, Chipping and Bolton-by-Bowland are as fair as any in the land.

The majority of walks are on rights of way or established access areas and paths: a handful which cross Open Access land are noted as such. Most days of the year you can freely walk here, but dogs are banned from grouse moors other than on rights of way. These areas can occasionally be closed, most likely from the grouse-shooting season's August start, though weekends should largely be unaffected: details from Natural England and information centres. Whilst the route description should be sufficient to guide you around, a map is recommended for greater information and interest: Ordnance Survey Explorer maps OL41 and 287 cover all the walks.

- Forest of Bowland AONB, Kettledrum, 6 Root Hill Estate Yard, Whitewell Road, Dunsop Bridge BB7 3AY (01200-448000)
- Bowland Visitor Centre, Beacon Fell Road, Goosnargh, Preston PR3 2EW (01995-640557)
- Visitor Information, Platform Gallery, Station Road, Clitheroe BB7 2JT (01200-425566)

RIBBLE VALLEY & BOWLAND
30 Short Scenic Walks

Shireburn Almshouse, Hurst Green

1   BOLTON PARK

3¼ miles from Bolton-by-Bowland

Gentle rambling on the edge of a lovely village

Start Village centre
(SD 785493; BB7 4NW), car park
Map OS Explorer OL41,
Forest of Bowland & Ribblesdale

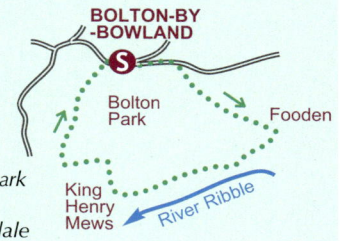

    Bolton-by-Bowland is a very attractive village boasting two greens, the smaller one with remains of a medieval cross and stocks. Here are the Coach & Horses pub, shop/tearoom, information room and WC. St Peter & St Paul's 15th century church tower is a splendid edifice of unfamiliar style. The church itself was rebuilt in 1852, but contains much older interest. In particular seek out the remarkable 1460s memorial to Sir Ralph Pudsay: 10ft long, it bears portraits of himself, 3 wives and 25 children carved in low relief. There is also a brass of Henry Pudsay (1509) and wife, while a 16th century font bears a more recent 'Mouseman' cover.

    From the centre head east on the main street past the church to the larger green. Keep on past the school and up the road rising out of the village. On a bend at a driveway, the adjacent kissing-gate sends you diagonally across a parkland pasture: a scant line of trees initially points the way to a kissing-gate ahead. Slant gently right up the field to a kissing-gate on the brow alongside the wood edge: Pendle Hill dominates ahead. Head way down a fenceside to the old farm at Fooden. A kissing-gate sends you down a small enclosure to a gate into the heart of the hamlet. On the left is a lovely cottage, and lower down the yard is 17th century Fooden Hall, with a two-storey gabled porch and mullioned windows.

    Opposite the cottage turn right between barns to a small corner gate, and bear right across an unkempt enclosure to the first of several kissing-gates. Advance along the field bottom with a part-sunken green way, in the next field running atop a wooded bank falling steeply to the Ribble Gorge. Though screened by trees the river is briefly glimpsed. At the next gate you emerge into open pasture above the gorge, running enclosed through new plantings. Emerging via a stile at the end, advance on down the fieldside to a kissing-gate and plank bridge at the end. Cross a large, sloping pasture to the next kissing-gate, with the buildings at King Henry Mews in view ahead. In front, take a small gate in the wall and turn right down the short access road to further houses. For more than four centuries Bolton Hall was home to the Pudsay family, but even its 1806 replacement was demolished in the 1960s.

Turn right on the driveway, and immediately after crossing a cattle-grid into Bolton Park, take a grass track left. It drops through a couple of kissing-gates onto the level and along to a footbridge and setted ford on Skirden Beck. Across, resume on a track upstream, quickly rising away to a kissing-gate. Just a little further, take one on the right and cross towards the bank above the beck. Continue outside trees to a corner stile, and resume outside the trees. When the wood swings right advance straight on to a stile in the hedge ahead. Rise left up a sheep pasture to merge with a fence. On the brow, just to the right is an old cross base under an oak tree. Drop with the fence to a wall-stile, meeting a driveway which runs left to Skirden Bridge at the village edge.

Bolton Park

2   AROUND SAWLEY

4¼ miles from Sawley

Open views and a delightful riverside between two villages

Start Village centre
(SD 776465; BB7 4NH),
roadside parking
Map OS Explorer OL41,
Forest of Bowland & Ribblesdale

Sawley is best known for Salley (old name) Abbey, founded by Cistercian monks in 1147. Small in scale and in the shadow of nearby Whalley Abbey, it suffered on more than one occasion from marauding Scots. The remains are in the care of English Heritage and open to the public. A lovely scene sees dabbling ducks on a green by the Spread Eagle pub, from where take the road downstream the short way to Sawley Bridge. The Ribble flows wide beneath its fine arches, with Penyghent and Fountains Fell seen far to the north. Just over the bridge is a junction. Turn briefly left, then right along a short drive to a cluster of dwellings with a former Friends' Meeting House of 1777 on the left.

At the end bear left up a short-lived cart track into the foot of a small wooded clough. A path takes over to rise through trees to a stile into a field at the top. Continue up to join a driveway and go left to a junction with an access road: big views look across the valley to Pendle Hill. Turn up the drive to various dwellings at Hill House Farm. Keep on over a cattle-grid on the main drive ahead, swinging left to enter a farmyard: pass right of the white farmhouse into a small paddock. Straight across are twin stiles in a hedge, then bear right to a gate at the field corner. Continue away along a fenceside, reaching a gate/stile just short of the end. Bear right to cross a reedy trickle in the field centre, then advance on to the tapering corner. Over the stile/slab bridge, rise to a gate/stile into the terminus of a green lane. Follow its broad, hedgerowed course up to join a driveway at two houses on the brow, and follow this away as it drops towards Grindleton. At a former Methodist Free Church of 1862 keep straight on to the main street just ahead.

Turn left down the footway to a junction at the bottom by the Duke of York pub (currently closed). Turn right to drop out of the village, and at the village sign a bridle-gate on the right sends a fieldside path downhill parallel with the road. Rejoining lower down, drop to a junction at scattered houses and bear left to approach Grindleton Bridge. Just before it a gate on the left accesses the riverbank for a lovely stroll upstream, some sections having succumbed to erosion. Several kissing-gates are encountered, and just beyond a confluence the embankment ends. From a kissing-gate a thin path bears left to another at an outer corner. Go right with the fence still shadowing the river, until reaching a sidestream bear left on its near side to a kissing-gate. With the head of a grassy lane on the left, instead go right a few yards over the stream and turn left up the fieldside above the tree-lined stream. From a stile at the top, cross a field centre to a wall-stile onto a road. Turn right past Bowland High School, soon dropping to a nice corner with woods, cottages and the river returning. From a stile on the right cross to another to rejoin the bank for a short stroll upstream back to a stile at Sawley Bridge.

Sawley Abbey

3   TWISTON BECK

3¾ miles from Downham

A charming ramble by beckside and delectable pastures

Start Village centre
(SD 785441; BB7 4BW), car park
Map OS Explorer OL41, Forest of Bowland & Ribblesdale (or OL21)

    Downham is a lovely village, with its street climbing to St Leonard's church with a 15th century tower: inside are monuments to the Assheton family whose arms adorn the pub across the road. At the foot of the village, ducks dabble in the stream overlooked by 16th century Old Well Hall. There is an information room/WC at the car park, and ice cream parlour close by. From the bridge climb the road towards the church. Above the pub turn right on a short drive above its car park, and at the end take a bridle-gate on the left. Ascend a short fieldside to a kissing-gate, then rise to a few trees on the brow of Downham Green. A clear day reveals the peaks of Ingleborough and Penyghent high in the Yorkshire Dales.

    Just as you start to descend, your unmarked way slants gently right. Through a steeper drop aim for limestone knolls to the right. Approaching them, what initially seems an isolated boulder is actually the base of an old cross. In front of the main tree-topped outcrop, descend left past smaller ones to a gate in a hedge. On the other side a drive leads right to Downham Mill. Now a private dwelling, the arch of this former corn mill's undershot waterwheel hole is prominent. Pass right of the house and out via a stile/gate at the rear, where a path heads away past the old millpond.

    Continue along the valley floor with Ings Beck until reaching a footbridge on it. Across, resume upstream to a kissing-gate, and although the right-of-way strictly climbs the bank and runs along the top, long-time usage traces the grassy path along the length of this beckside pasture to a plank bridge and stile at a sidestream at the end. Go right on a short boardwalk, and continue with the fence a short way to rejoin Ings Beck. A delightful path shadows it to a footbridge. Here bear right, with Twiston Beck below and Pendle Hill looming ahead. Ignoring a bridge down to the right, this lovely section leads through stiles and gates near meandering Twiston Beck to the former Twiston Mill: pass right of the fine barn grouping to a kissing-gate onto Twiston Lane.

Go briefly right until bridging the beck, then take a small gate on the left by the former mill-dam. A briefly enclosed path emerges into a field, on as far as a footbridge on the beck. Across, double back briefly then rise with an old hedgerow. From a gate/stile at the top head away with a hedge to the corner. A gate sends a briefly enclosed path into another field corner: turn right along the fieldside. Through a gate/stile at the end, a grassy path re-forms and drops gently down with a wall to a former quarry. From a stile on the right head away with a wall towards New Close Farm, but before the end take a kissing-gate on the left where the wall ends. Head away with a hedge, and when it drops away advance across the field to a footbridge at the end. Now bear right across a large field to a stile in a tiny section of wall opposite, before the end. Cross the field corner to an identical set-up on your right, then to a gate/stile just ahead. Now bear right to join Downham Beck, which leads pleasantly down past a spring to enter the village.

At Downham

4 PENDLE HILL

3¾ miles from Lane Head

A steep climb to the Ribble Valley's premier landmark, with priceless views

Start Lane Head (SD 797432; BB7 4BX), small parking area a mile south-east of Downham
Map OS Explorer OL41, Forest of Bowland & Ribblesdale (or OL21)
Access Open Access, dogs on leads

At the rear of the parking area a path rises to a kissing-gate for a steep, grassy climb with a colourful heathery clough on your right. From the outset you have magnificent views north across the Ribble Valley to the Yorkshire Dales, including Ingleborough, Penyghent and the Upper Wharfedale fells, while westwards are the Bowland moors beyond Waddington Fell and Downham. Higher, the going eases as a fence comes in to guide you up to a wall-stile onto the Open Access land of Downham Moor. With the flat skyline of the hill high above, the path rises intermittently moistly across rough moorland, easing out at a small boundary stone. On the steep slopes ahead are two near identical zigzags, the left one being your ascent route and the right one your return route.

After a gentle rise through a small gate in a fence, the path runs to the base of the steep upper slopes, where it bears left to the start of a sunken way. Ignoring a short-cut path in front, go left on this splendid old way, later slanting back across the hill to another bend. As the way swings back left, it maintains an unswerving, prolonged slant across the otherwise uniformly very steep fellside. Towards the end it swings further right to ease up on the higher slopes, running to a gate in a wall. Just to your right a stone shelter sits by the wall. The Ordnance Survey column on the summit is just ahead now, and you join a firm path rising the short way to the waiting top at 1827ft/557m. Just yards to its east, a perch on the rim of the mighty drop enjoys a bird's-eye view over Barley in its fold of the hills. Pendle's height and isolation ensure extensive views in all directions, with the South and West Pennine moors beyond East Lancashire's conurbations, Longridge Fell and the Bowland moors to the west, and a long Dales line-up to the north.

Commence the return by first returning to the gate, either the way you came or by a path along the rim to pick up the Barley ascent path by the wall. Through it, take a broad, grassy way bearing left between the diverging wall and your ascent path. This runs an excellent lengthy course across a gentle ridge, dipping slightly then over a minor brow to drop right to a ladder-stile in a wall. Don't cross, but double back sharply right on a thin, clear path running a near-level course along the rim, even revealing the summit, briefly, before reaching a fork. Here slant gently left to merge with a sunken way just short of a mini-clamber down through rocks at a former quarry. At its base you meet a level, grassy access track: go left on it beneath quarry scars, quickly beginning a sunken slant down Downham Moor. At a sharp bend double back right, and lower down it doubles back left to suddenly end. Slant right for a few pathless minutes across the moor to pick up the outward route in the vicinity of the fence-gate. Retrace opening steps, the lower pasture making a lovely finish as you take in that splendid northerly panorama.

Downham from Downham Moor

5 DOWNHAM LANDSCAPES

4¼ miles from Chatburn

Super paths to and from a classic village beneath Pendle Hill

Start Village centre
(SD 769441; BB7 4AU),
roadside parking
Map OS Explorer OL41, Forest of Bowland & Ribblesdale

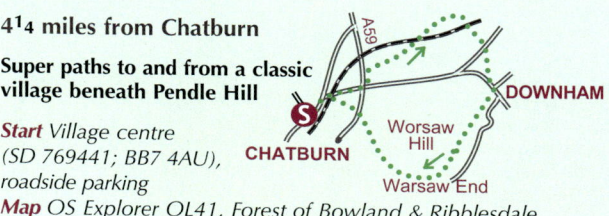

Chatburn has pubs, shops, a renowned ice cream parlour in the old toll house and a tall-spired church. Leave by the Downham road rising out of the village to bridge the deep A59 cutting. Across, take a gate left, and from another behind, a grass track drops gently away. Bearing right at the bottom, your path runs a lovely course enclosed in greenery. Bridging the railway it ultimately emerges into a field. Advance towards a barn, deflected round its right side by gates, and through a gate/stile at its other side continue with a wall on your right. From a kissing-gate drop by a hedge to a footbridge, across which the path crosses a pasture to the far corner. While your onward route is right, first use the wall-stile below to visit Swanside Bridge, a superb packhorse bridge on Smithies Brook.

Back at the stile ascend outside New Field Wood, turning left at the top to a rail underpass. Now bear right up the field to a gate above, then follow a wallside track up to a kissing-gate onto a road. Go right to a stile hidden in the hedge on the left just after a kink, then bear right up the pasture of Downham Green to an ascending wall. Follow this over the brow to approach Downham, and drop down with the wall to a kissing-gate. Descend a fieldside to a bridle-gate, then right on a short drive to emerge at the top of the village. For a note on Downham see page 10.

Descend the street, and from the bridge at the bottom turn right on a side road to the car park entrance. Between road and entrance, turn up a short drive to a couple of houses. From a stile by a gate between them, head off with a fence on the right, becoming briefly enclosed. Emerging into a field, advance on through a gate and rise away outside Longlands Wood, with Pendle Hill rising majestically ahead. At the end is a stile/gate: with the limestone knoll of Worsaw Hill ahead, bear left across a large field to a stile/gate in the far corner. Entering the field on your right, advance above a hedge to a stile/gate ahead. A path heads away above a wall on the base of Worsaw Hill. Shortly you pass above Worsaw End House, setting for the 1960s film 'Whistle Down the Wind'.

The path slants slightly right to remain on the base of the hill, winding round beneath a scrubby bank. Swinging right again, a gentle rise leads to a brow with limestone outcrops looking to Pendle Hill, Longridge Fell and Bowland. The continuing path drops to a small gate, then slants down a scrubby limestone bank and on to a corner stile. Head away, dropping to a kissing-gate at the edge of the A59. Turn right on a parallel path until it rises to the road, which cross with care. Steps down the other side send an enclosed streamside path away to approach a driveway. Go left over a footbridge, across the drive and briefly along an enclosed path to reach wall-stiles on either side. From that on the right descend an outer garden to a bridge back over the stream, then cross a drive to steps up to a tall gate onto an access road at the end of a long terrace. Go left past a Methodist church out onto the road, with the centre just down to the left.

Pendle Hill from under Worsaw Hill

6   WEST BRADFORD FELL

4¾ miles from West Bradford

A sustained, easy climb from pasture to fellside: big views

Start *Village centre (SD 744445; BB7 4SX), roadside parking (village hall car park on Grindleton road)*
Map *OS Explorer OL41, Forest of Bowland & Ribblesdale*

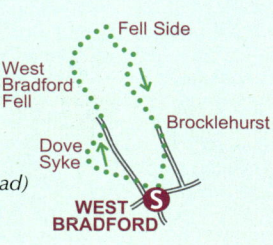

At the head of the main street turn left on the Waddington road, passing the Three Millstones pub and rising above the brook out of the village. Here take an unsigned byway right, running above the brook and passing an old Methodist burial ground. The track swings left up onto Eaves Hall Lane beneath Eaves Hall Hotel. Go right a few strides to a flight of steps left up into a garden edge. Cross to a kissing-gate, then advance across a field centre the short way to a plank bridge. Follow a fence on the right just as far as a gateway in it, then ascend a large field to buildings above. A stile left of the first house puts you onto a drive. From one opposite, advance outside the second house and bear left to a stile/gate just ahead. Ascend the next two field centres to the houses at Dove Syke: a stile leads to a short enclosed way between them. On the drive, turn right as far as the end of trees on your left. As a nursery access road comes in, take a stile on the left and slant to the top of a line of trees. From a stile/slab bridge resume the slant towards houses at Hancocks. A stile/gate admits onto surfaced Moor Lane.

Turn uphill until it swings left to Seedalls Farm: here take the gate in front to ascend a cart track to a barn. A little higher the sometimes unkempt way becomes enclosed, and settles down as a gently ascending green track. Gradients ease as you run between rough moor-grass pastures, and the track kinks right to quickly reach a second bend. Instead of passing through the gate to continue up, take a gateway on the right and head off on another grassy wallside way, narrowing to a path. Through a gate it rises onto heather-clad moor with the now crumbling wall over a gentle brow: at 1000ft/305m on Sour Dock Hill the walk's summit has views north into the Yorkshire Dales. Path and wall drop to the old farm at Fell Side: without entering, turn right on the wallside green way. From a gate at the end advance a short way on a thinner trod to be faced with a wall-kink on a grassy knoll amid bracken.

The thin path swings left down this steeper, bracken pasture alongside a reedy hollow, then doubles back to a gateway in the bottom corner. Now pathless, drop left with a fence to the bottom, then bear right a little before crossing the marshy stream. Across, slant gently right up the bank and cross to a gate where wall and fence meet. Heading away with a wall, a grassy track forms to lead down through two lengthy pastures to a gate onto a surfaced drive. Continue down to Brocklehurst Farm (a house), and take a gate/stile on the right into a large field just past the head of a wooded stream. Head away, parallel with Drakehouse Wood to a gate in a fence at a dry stream crossing. Slant left down to a gateway, then right, passing above an outer hedge corner. Continue through a scant line of hawthorns and down to the foot of a driveway just above a farm. This leads down through the yard and onto the road in the village.

At West Bradford Fell

7   EASINGTON FELL

4 miles from Waddington Fell

A high-altitude stride over colourful moorland slopes

Start B6478 road summit (SD 718480; BB7 3AA), parking area   *Access* Open Access, see page 4
Map OS Explorer OL41, Forest of Bowland & Ribblesdale

Head along the broad verge away from the cattle-grid, quickly dropping to Walloper Well where springs pour into roadside troughs. Two minutes further is a lay-by where a grassy track doubles back right across a moist streamlet to commence a slant up the moor. Almost at once on your right is the site of a dam that served a lead smelting mill. Reaching a major fork at a small boundary stone, ignore the main way curving left, and keep right to stride across, then gently up, the grassy moor. At a ladder-stile in a wall, don't cross but take a thinner way rising left. This quickly eases to trace the wall along to the top edge of Grindleton Forest. A boundary stone bears the initials of Grindleton, West Bradford and Newton. Just beyond, a branch slants left the two minutes to Easington Fell's cairn at 1299ft/396m. This mass of fell you are tramping has any number of names depending on which part you're currently on: though Waddington Fell is widely used, Easington Fell narrowly claims its summit. The panorama stretches from Longridge Fell round via the Bowland moors to Yorkshire's Three Peaks.

Back at the boundary stone, step over the fence-gate behind and a thin path descends outside the forest fence. Dropping faintly through heather and two crumbled walls, a bigger drop is revealed as the forest turns off left at an old wall: Pendle Hill rises across the valley. Turn right on the path beneath the wall, just 100 yards to a branch left: joined by another, it drops to a sturdy cairn just below. The path then slants left through bracken down to a cross-paths at the forest edge. The wallside path to your right will be your return route. Descend the colourful path outside the trees to a bridle-gate at a junction with an enclosed green way from the right: you shall return here after a lower loop. Continue down outside the trees, and beyond a bridle-gate a firmer forest road comes in. Just a little further down, by a couple of trees at some scant ruins, take a grassy path right. It passes between the ruins and swings right up through an old wall, then left on a level course across the rough grass. A gate/stile in an old wall comes after bridging a streamlet above a plantation. Bear gently left on a thin trod, quickly merging with an old wall and encountering a moist spell before rising slightly to a wall junction with the shell of Fell Side to your left.

Turn right on a grassy wallside trod to a bridle-gate onto a walled green way. Turn right for a direct march rising gently back to the forest-edge. Through the bridle-gate return up the path to the corner where forest and moor meet. This time take the inviting path left through Bradford Fell's bracken, slightly above the wall. Rising gently away, it curves right to a cross-paths at two stone gateposts: keep left on the path aiming for Waddington Fell's mast. Quickly trading bracken for increasing heather, this runs a largely excellent course over a gentle brow. Slowly leaving heather behind, it drops to run to a gate in a wall. Through it a green track makes a bee-line for the road summit in front of Waddington Fell Quarry. From a stile onto the road turn right over the cattle-grid to finish.

On Bradford Fell, looking to Pendle Hill

8   RIBBLE AT WADDINGTON

4 miles from Waddington

Good Ribble-side paths between two fine bridges close by a classic village

Start *Village centre (SD 728439; BB7 3HZ), roadside parking (playing fields car park on Bashall Eaves road)*
Map *OS Explorer OL41, Forest of Bowland & Ribblesdale*

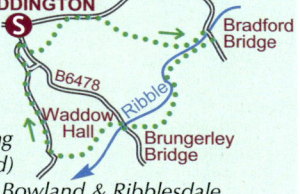

Waddington is a showpiece village with a charming stream. There are three pubs, tearoom, Post office/shop and WC. St Helen's church retains its solid tower of 1501, while inside are a 15th century font and medieval glass. The 'Hospital' is a delightful arrangement of almshouses founded 300 years ago. Turn down the main street to the war memorial gardens, noting Waddington Old Hall on the left. Restored a century ago, much of it dates back over 500 years. Here take a dark snicket left to emerge into a field, with Pendle Hill dominant to your right. Head across the centre, bearing left to a far corner stile onto a road on the village edge.

Go right on the footway to the school, and ignoring a path through a kissing-gate opposite, advance a few yards further to Healings Farm. Immediately after it take an enclosed path right, emerging at the end via a stile into a field. Cross to successive crude fence-stiles, then bear right over this field corner to a more obvious one just ahead. Advance to the edge of a colourful hollow, a path dropping to cross its part marshy floor to ascend a wooden stairway. Over the slight brow drop to a fence-stile, with the massive cement works as backdrop. Bear right across the field to another stile, then on again to drop right through successive kissing-gates in undergrowth. Cross one last field corner onto the bank of the River Ribble, and turn upstream to the waiting three arches of Bradford Bridge: steps take you up onto the road.

Across, take an easily missed stile on the right to resume downstream, a good path faithfully tracing the river to a bend where you enter the trees of Cross Hill Quarry nature reserve. The path rises to join a level one, going right with it amid various sculptures. A little further you see the old quarry face set back to the left. Beyond, you are deflected up a bank to follow a hard, higher-level path through trees. Ignoring any left branches, the way drops back towards the river to run on to the B6478 at Brungerley Bridge. Turn right to cross the impressive bridge. Built in the early 19th century, it is inscribed with townships and the real counties it divides: 'Clitheroe, Lancashire; Waddington, Yorkshire'.

Across, rise briefly up the footway then take a kissing-gate on the left. An old drive heads away, quickly merging with the present one to go left to approach Waddow Hall. Dating from Tudor times, it has been substantially enlarged and serves as a girl guide centre. Over a crossroads on a brow, drop to a cattle-grid where your path is deflected right up around the wall enclosing the grounds. It drops back down at the far end to an old carriageway, which follow right. This pleasant parkland track has views to Longridge Fell and Parlick, with Waddington Fell re-appearing. At a kissing-gate onto a road turn right to return to the village. As the Lower Buck Inn appears ahead, a wall-stile on the right offers a field finish, crossing to a small gate into the streamside gardens.

The Ribble at Bradford Bridge

9   GREAT MITTON

4½ miles from Clitheroe

Easy Ribble-side walking between two old bridges

Start Edisford Bridge (SD 727414; BB7 3LJ), car park a mile out of town on B6243
Map OS Explorer OL41, Forest of Bowland & Ribblesdale

From the car park join the road, where a path runs down to the riverside. Cross the bridge (with the Edisford Bridge Inn just beyond) and turn down the open bank: this opening section is a concessionary path. Just short of the end of the open area, take a kissing-gate on the right and a path runs left, rising with a fence to a kissing-gate in the top corner. Turn left on a broad path through woodland, emerging through a gate at the end. Join the riverbank for a delectable stroll downstream through a sweeping pasture.

From a stile at the end, a stepped path climbs the wooded bank to a kissing-gate, from where cross the field to the right of a waterworks building. Continue to a corner stile onto its access track, and a gate on your right puts you onto a junction of ways. Cross straight over the access road to a stile ahead, to the left. Now go left on the fieldside, to a stile at the end and on by a streamlet immersed in scrub. Continue to a stile ahead, near a confluence to the left. The lesser stream leads on to a bridge over it to a stile behind. Entering a vast field, bear steadily left to merge with the hedge. A little beyond a hollowed pool, a kissing-gate puts you onto an old green way, Malkin Lane: turn right on its enclosed course to Church Lane in Great Mitton. Turn left, winding round to a junction in this tiny village with the derelict Three Fishes pub to the right. All Hallows church dates from the 14th century: inside is a pre-Reformation screen from Sawley Abbey, while the Shireburn chapel of 1594 boasts numerous recumbent effigies. At the junction go left past the church and historic Mitton Hall, down the road to cross Mitton Bridge. The Ribble glides over rocky shelves downstream, while upstream it leads the eye to Pendle Hill: note also the fine setting of the hall and church.

At the bridge end is the Aspinall Arms, past which a kissing-gate sends you along the field edge, gently up to a wooded bank above the river. Through a kissing-gate on the brow a further fieldside leads down to another such gate, and a grassy path down to a footbridge on a sidestream. Entering a large riverside pasture, cross to a small building from where a grassy track leads upstream to an aqueduct: a broad riverside track now runs to Shuttleworth Farm. Passing left of the buildings, a pair of kissing-gates send a path across a small paddock to meet the drive as it leaves the farm. Follow this out past several houses, continuing upstream beneath a screened refuse site: here the river leaves. Your road heads straight on, absorbing the 'tip' road. Just past Mill House, a casual path slips into trees to pleasantly trace the beck upstream. The road is rejoined at a stone-arched bridge, just past which turn left on Siddows Farm drive. At the early fork, go right a few yards then take a bridle-gate on the left, an enclosed path curving round a small field to overlook the Ribble again at the far corner. The path slants down to the river, and runs firmly upstream to the start, passing a caravan site and a miniature railway and WC.

Great Mitton church

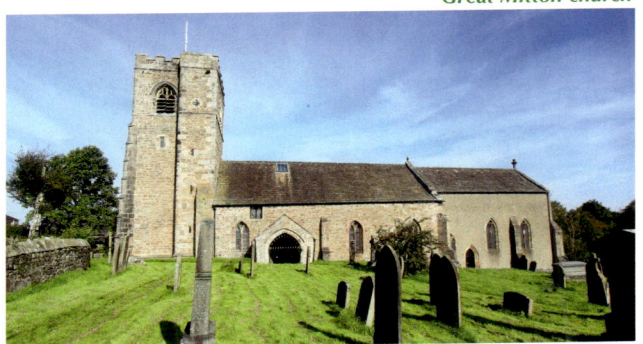

10   NICK OF PENDLE

4 miles from Pendleton

A fine moorland stroll on the flanks of Pendle Hill

Start *Village centre
(SD 755395; BB7 1PT), car park*
Map *OS Explorer OL41,
Forest of Bowland & Ribblesdale*

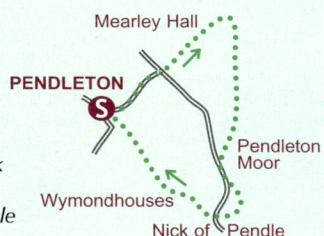

Pendleton is an attractive linear village with a stream through the centre and the Swan with Two Necks pub. On a tiny green is Fiddle Bridge, returned to the village in 2000 after 200 years absence. Take the road rising out, which leaves by swinging left between the old National School and All Saints church. With Pendle Hill's flanks above, it runs to a T-junction at a small green. Cross to a farm road at Pendleton Hall and head away, opening out between fields to approach the old house of Mearley Hall. Just short of the grounds, turn right up a fenceside to a gate/stile. An enclosed path rises by a stream, quickly emerging into a field corner. Crossing a streamlet on your right, slant slightly right up this large field, close by the stream on your left. Reaching a roofless barn at the top, to the left behind it is a ladder-stile onto grassy Mearley Moor.

Bearing off right across the moor, a trod forms beyond reeds, running a level course to pass through hummocks to approach Ashendean Clough. Views look over the Ribble Valley to Longridge Fell, Bowland's moors and Waddington Fell. Aiming for Howcroft Barn in the field ahead, drop to find a footbridge beneath a small wood. Across, rise left with the wall to remain on the moor, around to a gate in an intervening fence. Continue with the wall, rising slightly across Pendleton Moor. Before long, and just before the wall's high point, bear left on an improving trod rising still very gently. Its pleasant course crosses two broader paths to run a level course to join the Clitheroe-Sabden road at a parking area.

Turn up the verge the short way to Wellsprings restaurant/cafe alongside Pendle Ski Club's dry slopes. Turn left up a part-sunken way just short of the Wellsprings, curving pleasantly right to meet a wide path on the broad moorland ridge - the walk's summit. Views ahead reveal a long line of South Pennines, while Clitheroe sits in the valley to your right beneath a Bowland skyline. Turn right along the ridge for a gentle descent to the road summit at the Nick of Pendle, at 985ft/300m a popular start point for Pendle Hill's ascent.

Cross with care and go briefly right to a wall-stile. A path slants down reedy pasture to merge with a wall opposite, dropping to a corner gate/stile. Behind, a track drops right to quickly join a solid wall heading for Wymondhouses. Part way down, a small gate in it sends a thin path slanting left down towards the house. In an unkempt corner to its right is a small gate, with a wall-stile behind. Head directly away through a further gate and along a hedgeside: just short of the bottom take a gate on the right. Head away with a hedge to a gate/stile, then turn sharp left to resume the descent. Passing through a tree-line bear right to drop to a footbridge in the far corner. Resume down the other side of the tree-lined stream, a long, tapering field leading to a gate by a house at the very end. Its short access road joins the road by the church at the head of the village.

Looking west from Pendleton Moor

11   DEERSTONES

4½ miles from Sabden

A bracing moorland tramp on Pendle Hill's southern flank

Start *Village centre (SD 779393; BB7 9DZ), car park*
Map *OS Explorer 287, West Pennine Moors*

Sabden is a pleasant village with the White Hart and Pendle Witch pubs, café and shops. From the central crossroads turn right on Wesley Street for St Nicholas' church with its thin, slender spire, but before it take a lane left for Badger Wells Cottages. Rising to Cockshotts Farm, go left over a stream up to the front of the cottages. To their right an enclosed path rises to a gate at the top, with Deerstones breaking the skyline. An inviting path heads up the pasture, through a kissing-gate at the top corner to resume above Badger Well Water. Grand strides lead up through an intervening gate to a kissing-gate onto the foot of grassy moor.

The path rises a little further to meet a track: turn right on it, using gates to pass briefly through a field-top to rejoin the moor. With Churn Clough Reservoir below, it rises gently away from the wall to reach a tree-lined stream. Winding up the bank opposite it runs on again to a kissing-gate above a replanted plantation. Rising gently again above an old wall, you arrive above a short drop to another streamlet beneath new plantings. Across, the path leaves the plantation behind and swings uphill, initially through bracken, on a sustained climb alongside a fence enclosing the deep clough. As the fence turns off, the path curves right to pleasantly scale the broad shoulder falling from Deerstones. Gaining the grassy edge, the main path goes ahead towards a wall: instead make use of a thinner right branch scaling the grassy edge to quickly reach its high point at around 1410ft/430m. The minor outcrops make a fine halting place overlooking a deep, bouldery amphitheatre.

Resume by retracing a few steps before branching right on a thin trod slanting down towards the wall, joining a level path and merging with the ascent path just in front of a gate. A good path heads away, initially level then dropping and curving left: ignore a cross-path just prior to merging into the wide Pendle Hill path on its broad ridge. Go left for a good stride down this prolonged, gentle decline all the way to the 985ft/300m road summit at the Nick of Pendle. During this spell Clitheroe is seen down to the right beneath Waddington Fell, backed by the Bowland moors.

Go left down the verge just as far as an easily missed gate set back on the right. Note the easiest conclusion simply follows the road back down into the village, utilising parallel paths on this slender strip of open country. The full route follows a drive away to Parsley Barn, after which bear off left down an unkempt pasture to a gate/stile at the reedy bottom. Drop to and quickly cross a gorse-lined streamlet to reach a wall, re-crossing the stream to a wallside path. Through a gate/stile it drops by the wooded gill, soon swinging more broadly right down to the far end of buildings at The Whins. From a gate on the left pass along the front of the first and then on an enclosed green way to a driveway between houses. Go briefly right, then from a wall-stile on the left a path heads off along the field bottom, rising slightly at the end to a kissing-gate. A thinner way resumes, again rising slightly to run to a gate onto the road at the village edge. Go right down the footway to finish.

Ascending to Deerstones

12   WHALLEY BANKS

4¾ miles from Whalley

Richly varied rambling around the environs of the River Calder

Start Town centre
(SD 733361; BB7 9SP)
Map OS Explorer 287,
West Pennine Moors

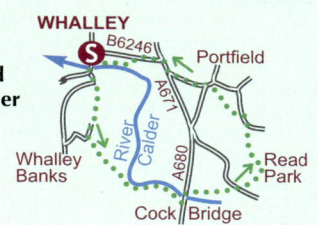

Whalley is best known for its Cistercian abbey, entered through a gatehouse of 1480: finer still is a 14th century gatehouse over a road. St Mary & All Saints' church has a Norman doorway and 15th century stalls. From King Street walk south to cross Whalley Bridge on the River Calder, looking downstream to a massive 1850 rail viaduct. Turn sharp left up Moor Lane, climbing steeply to an early bend where a sunken bridleway climbs left to a viewpoint above the river. Here take the left-hand path rising parallel with the bridleway through a sliver of woodland, offering open views over the valley. Merging at the corner of Nab Wood, go straight ahead on the sunken bridleway climbing to an access road. Advance to houses ahead, and straight on between them to a gate. A leafy way runs to the larger grouping of houses at Whalley Banks.

Keep straight on until the access road climbs right, then take a short drive in front. Once again path and bridleway run parallel here: take the path on the left to soon emerge via a kissing-gate into a field with big views to moors beyond Burnley. The thin path winds down to a tree-lined stream, soon crossing it at a kissing-gate. An enclosed course with the stream leads to another such gate where you briefly re-cross, then down a little further to a slab bridge. Head away across a sloping pasture above the Calder, then drop gently left to approach Dean Brook. A path re-forms to cross a slab bridge to a kissing-gate into trees, then climbs steps to run above the steep, wooded riverbank. From a kissing-gate at the end the path runs more freely and grandly above the trees. A path then descends to the bank, crossing a sidestream for a superb riverbank stroll. Across another footbridge you are deflected from the river by a part wooded bank, rising across the field to a kissing-gate onto the A680. To the right is the Game Cock pub.

Turn left on the footway to cross Cock Bridge, then right on a drive to a garden centre/tearoom. At its entrance take a firm track rising left beneath Cock Wood to the A671. Cross with care to a lodge and ascend a drive through Read Park. At Coppy Plantation at the top turn left off the forking drive to a gate/stile, and a track heads away outside the wood. After an intervening gate it runs on to a pair of gates at the wood end. From a stile by the left one a better grass track continues, meeting another wood then slowly angling away from it down a large pasture onto a road at Read Old Bridge. Just up the other side take a farm drive left, but quickly leave by a stile on the right. Ascend directly to the brow, then on to a stile/gate ahead. Cross the next field to another, then bear right to a stile across a smaller field. Up another brow cross to a stile by the right-hand house, onto a road junction at Portfield. Cross to go left down Portfield Road onto the A671. Go right to cross at traffic lights by Spring Wood car park, and descend the B6246's footway. At the 'Whalley' sign, take a path left to drop down to the river. This leads pleasantly downstream, and at a weir joins a back street back into town.

River Calder at Whalley

13   RIBBLE WOODLANDS

4¼ miles from Salesbury

Easy rambling through beautiful riverside scenery

Start Marles Wood
(SD 676356; PR3 3XU),
car park above Salesbury Hall
Map OS Explorer 287, *West Pennine Moors*

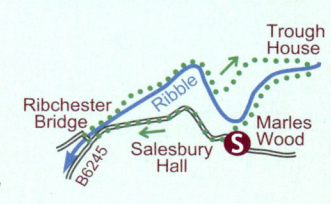

Rejoin the road and turn right down through the wood, quickly levelling out to wind on past modern developments at Salesbury Hall. A lengthy, level hedgerowed course then runs on past a caravan park and Ribbleside House to reach Ribchester Bridge on the River Ribble. On the left is the former De Tabley Arms, recalling an important land-owning family, while two minutes further is New Hall, a fine 17th century house. Ribchester Bridge with its three graceful arches dates from 1774. Cross and turn upstream on a farm drive, with Pendle Hill far ahead. The drive leaves the river part way along to reach Dewhurst House. Entering the yard, turn down to the right to find a short-lived path running to a gate/stile accessing the riverbank in a lovely setting.

The grassy path turns upstream, staying generally close to the river. Passing beneath Stewart's Wood the main path forks left up the bank, dropping back to enter Haugh Wood at a kissing-gate/footbridge as the river undertakes a great sweep. A glorious woodland section ensues on the bank, and just before the end the path swings left up to a kissing-gate out of the trees. Climb the small bank into a rolling field, and head directly away across the centre of this extensive pasture. On the brow you are greeted by a super prospect of Pendle Hill beyond a sweep of the river. Now swing sharp left to a gate/stile in a dip, then bear left across the pasture, soon swinging uphill to a gate/stile at the far corner above a wood. Cross a small enclosure to a bridle-gate onto a driveway above the isolated house at Hey Hurst.

A few steps down the drive, a bridle-gate opposite sends you off down a hedgeside, with a glimpse back to the late 17th century house. Lower down you descend outside a wood to a footbridge on Starling Brook. From it head away with a hedge on your right, along the bottoms of several fields until the adjacent fence parts company. With Dinckley footbridge seen over to the right, keep straight on to a gate ahead, sending a short enclosed track through trees. Just short of Trough House Farm, a bridle-gate on the right sends a short, enclosed path doubling back to the bridge. Cross in style on this substantial bridge, enjoying lovely views both up and down river. A suspension bridge erected in 1951 to replace a ferry suffered storm damage in 2015, and this new replacement opened in 2019. The far bank is the place to take in the verdant scene, with sandy banks and a series of scars interrupting the water's flow.

Turn downstream along open pastures with the river partly obscured by trees, at the end revealing a smashing prospect as the Ribble glides between richly wooded banks. Entering Marles Wood, a broad path heads away above the river, and at the far end the rocks of Coppy Scar call for a further halt. This aggressively attractive section of river features the whirlpool of Sale Wheel, before it turns away for contrastingly lazy sweeps. Your path bears left to remain in the trees, and at an early fork a concessionary path climbs directly to the car park.

The Ribble below Sale Wheel

14 RIBCHESTER DEWPONDS

4¼ miles from Ribchester

Old dewponds scattered by fieldpaths above a Roman site

Start Village centre (SD 650351; PR3 3XP), car park
Map OS Explorer 287, West Pennine Moors

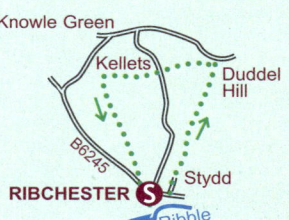

Ribchester Roman fort guarded a river crossing on the road north from Manchester: a Roman Museum tells more. St Wilfrid's church has a 14th century tower and 1735 box pews. Along with the Black Bull and White Bull pubs are a tearoom and Post office/shop. From the end of the main street above the river a path goes left past the school, with a big prospect of the wide-flowing Ribble. Swinging left with Stydd Brook you pass a small gate accessing a Roman bath-house, then shortly cross a track onto the open space of Greenside featuring a war memorial of 2014. Joining a back road, turn right to a junction opposite the Ribchester Arms. Go right past it then left on Stydd Lane, rising to an interesting corner featuring St Peter & St Paul's Catholic church of 1789 and Stydd Almshouses, built in 1728 by the Shireburns of Stonyhurst.

Continue up the drive past 12th century St Saviours' church to a farm, Stydd Manor. Head straight up the yard to emerge into a field, and a track rises with a hedge on the right. At the top use a stile by the right-hand gate, then up with a hedge on the left. Over a footbridge at the top ascend a large pasture to a gate/stile along the top, with a dry dewpond to the left. Made to quench cattle's thirst, it is the first of several: higher to the left is a mast. The climb ends on Duddel Hill just ahead, with views to Longridge Fell and Pendle Hill. Advance past modern barns to a gate at Duddel House, and follow the drive out to the B6243. However, before the cattle-grid take a stile on the left and cross the field to another, continuing to one into a massive field. As it falls away at the end, drop to a footbridge on Stydd Brook, and a thin path slants up the opposite bank. Crossing a streamlet, rise to a stile into an outer garden alongside Cox Farm to a tiny corner gate onto a road.

Go briefly right to a stile on the left, and cross to a gateway in a hedge at a tree-shrouded dewpond. Through the next gateway bear right to a corner stile onto an access road. Cross straight over to reach another stile, then bear slightly right to the end of a row of trees. A track forms to join a firmer one with Kellets Farm to the right. Go left on this driveway to a house at Hazel Grove, just past which is a stile/gate. Bear right past an old dewpond to quickly drop to a stile. A path briefly runs through a wooded section to a footbridge, then bear right up the other side to a corner gate/stile. A fenceside cart track heads away to a gate/stile at the end.

Descending a massive sloping pasture with a ditch on your left, shortly cross it on a little path to a stile. Heading away, slant down to a stile at a tree-lined stream, then rise left to resume past another old pond. Remain with the left-hand boundary to curve right, down past another old pond to a corner stile. Resume down a fieldside, crossing an old access track to a gate/stile below. Resume down through another, then a pleasant little path crosses a longer pasture to its tapering end alongside Boyce's Brook. Over a bridge cross to a kissing-gate at the edge of modern housing on the site of Ribblesdale Mill. An enclosed cart track runs out onto a road on the village edge: go left to finish.

Stydd Almshouses

15   UNDER LONGRIDGE

4¼ miles from Hurst Green

Rural rambling featuring two fine old houses

Start Village centre (SD 685379; BB7 9QB), village hall car park
Map OS Explorer 287, West Pennine Moors

For a note on Hurst Green see page 36. From the war memorial opposite the Shireburn Arms head along Avenue Road to the Bayley Arms. Note just a few yards further the Shireburn Almshouse, with imposing semi-circular steps. From the pub, slant left down a drive opposite. Passing right of garages at the bottom, a woodland path runs to another drive: drop to the house and pass right on a path into woodland. With Dean Brook for company a broader path is soon joined, and the ensuing stage is a wonderful stroll amid nice woodland and water scenery. Stone-arched Sandy Bridge leads over the brook: note the waterslides upstream. The way then rises left, out along the top of the trees and into open surrounds. The path rises delightfully between enclosing greenery, merging into a drive rising to Greengore. Its intriguing architecture includes novel buttresses: dating back several centuries it was once a hunting lodge.

Keep straight on, right of the buildings, and as the track ends at a bridle-gate, a good path continues up the wallside outside the wood. This runs on beyond the wood through colourful surrounds, then via a bridle-gate along the edge of a new plantation on the left. From a gate at the end cross straight over a track onto a vague path slanting up rough pasture, aiming for a skyline ladder-stile between clumps of trees. Look back over richly-wooded country to the cupolas of Stonyhurst College, with Pendle Hill rising beyond. Head away above the wood on your left, on beneath a gorse bank to be deflected slightly right alongside a hedge. This leads along to a gate/stile at the end onto a road.

Turn left to descend past Huntingdon Hall, a splendid house of 1619. At the houses at Lane Ends, turn left on Carlinghurst drive. Just short of the buildings leave by a tiny gate on the left, then along outside the confines to another such gate. A fenced path runs on past a tiny plantation on your right, though the field on your left is shown as woodland on the map. Through a final small gate at the end, bear right to join a rough track. Go left on this across a field to a gate on the brow: from the adjacent stile, bear right around the field edge to a stile in the fence. Across, head away down the fieldside to join an access road at Lower Hud Lee.

Cross to a short access road, and along the front of the second house to a wall-stile ahead. A short-lived green way leads to a gate into a vast sloping field. Head away over a gentle knoll and all the way along to find a stile at the very end, at the right edge of a wood. Over a small footbridge, bear right to another footbridge in the corner. Rise to a stile just above, then climb left of distinctive tree-crowned Doe Hill and on beneath an Ordnance Survey column at 472ft/144m. Just beyond it locate a stile in the hedge slightly to the right onto an access road at a house. Go right, down to join a back road. Turn left, dropping to cross Dean Brook on the village edge and up the other side back to the Bayley Arms.

Bayley Arms, Hurst Green

16   STONYHURST COLLEGE

3¾ miles from Hurst Green

A charming riverbank approach to an elegant landscape

Start Village centre (SD 685379; BB7 9QB), village hall car park
Map OS Explorer 287, West Pennine Moors

Hurst Green is a pleasant village around a wide junction, with two pubs and WC. There is a war memorial on the green, and also a much less common Boer War memorial. From the main war memorial, cross the main road and turn into the car park of the Shireburn Arms: this recalls the family that owned Stonyhurst, with which the village is indelibly linked. Descend to a gate/stile and down the field with a hedge on the right: views over the valley feature Pendle Hill and Whalley Nab. When the fence turns off right, cross the streamlet and resume on a well-defined tongue between streams. At the bottom a path crosses two footbridges in succession, then bears left on an enclosed course outside the wood to a bridle-gate at the end. The path descends through woodland, dropping left to a bridge over a sidestream. Beyond this the riverbank is gained, and the Ribble followed upstream, quickly passing a substantial aqueduct.

The riverbank is traced for a little under a mile through occasional gates or stiles, until joining Jumbles farm drive. Here leave the river and turn left on to a site of light industry at Fox Fields: remain on the drive going right into woodland. Reaching a cottage, take a gate/stile on the left and ascend the field with a tree-lined streamlet to its demise just short of the top. Just ahead is a hedge-stile onto the B6243. Turn briefly left on its footway, then cross to a gate from where a hedgeside track rises away, passing New Barn to become enclosed and firmer underfoot to rise to Hall Barn Farm. Continue straight up the road ahead to approach Stonyhurst College. At a bend just before the wood on the left a gate is your route of departure, but first advance a little further to savour the delights of the college. First sighting is the chapel, with the South front to the right. Ahead are the West front and the ponds.

In its beautiful setting Stonyhurst College has long been a leading Roman Catholic boys' school that now takes girls too. The original house began in the late 14th century: the Elizabethan manor house was started by Sir Richard Shireburn, and the gatehouse dates from 1592. It was handed to the Society of Jesus in 1794, and 19th century extensions include the West front and the gatehouse. St Peter's church dates from 1835. Facing the West front are two ponds beloved of waterfowl, flanking St Nicholas' Avenue created between 1690 and 1717. The school contains a museum with religious artefacts dating back to the Reformation.

Back at the gate head off along a long, narrow field, later transferring to the wooded side to curve round past the wood-end, over a stream embankment and up to a kissing-gate. Rise to the next such gate, then up to a third. Here a short enclosed path winds around onto an access road, following it out past houses into the village. Go left past the Shireburn Almshouse with arms, inscriptions and fine semi-circular steps, and the village hall and Bayley Arms back into the centre.

Stonyhurst College

17 THREE RIVERS

4 miles from Lower Hodder Bridge

Easy rambling as the Ribble absorbs two major rivers

Start B6243 at bridge
(SD 704391; BB7 9PN), verge parking along from east side
(alternative start at junction to west)
Map OS Explorer 287, West Pennine Moors

Immediately downstream of the bridge is the remarkable 16th century Cromwell's Bridge, so named as the historical figure came this way prior to the Battle of Preston in 1648: a little path on the other side gives access. From the west side of the bridge follow the roadside footway as it curves up the hill, and just past a house on the left, cross to a gate set back. Rise away with a tree-lined streamlet and up to a stile in the hedge at the top. Turn right on the road, levelling out and quickly acquiring a footway. Approaching some buildings, take a broad drive left to Hall Barn Farm. Don't enter the yard, but keep straight ahead on a rough road to a junction of ways. To your right is Stonyhurst College, visited on Walk 16. Here go straight ahead on an access track past sports fields. As the main track swings right to a cricket pavilion, take the left branch dropping down to a gate/kissing-gate, then along to houses at Fair Field. Go left down their short drive onto the B6243.

Cross straight over and down the farm drive to Cross Gills, passing through to a gate by the last barn at the end and out on an initially enclosed track. This winds down beneath a cross on a knoll, with a 19th century shaft in an older base. From a stile by the right-hand of two gates at the bottom, advance on the grassy hedgeside track to meet the River Ribble. Turn left through a gate to trace the river upstream, quickly joining Jumbles farm drive. Keep right on the access road past the house and upstream to a hut alongside Jumbles Rocks. Ahead appears Hacking Hall, whose five gables date from 1607: the fact that it stands on the opposite bank is not, at this stage, apparent. Leave the drive at a kissing-gate to rejoin the bank in a lush pasture, and a big loop of the river ensues.

The isolated house to your left is a boatman's house from when the modest Hacking Ferry plied the river into the 1950s. A confluence with the River Calder is reached at a sharp bend of the river, a sandy beach at your feet being a perfect vantage point for the old hall. Resume upstream, superb riverside rambling leading to an anglers' refuge where a farm track forms. This leads along to Winckley Hall Farm. Just prior to its grounds a seat occupies an idyllic viewpoint overlooking a second, greater confluence, this time with the River Hodder. While the Ribble turns away with Pendle Hill directly behind, you resume briefly above the lovely Hodder before the track becomes enclosed to reach the farm. Turn left into the yard, then right opposite the house and out past an L-shaped pond, the remains of a moat.

Rise up the drive past the grounds of Winckley Hall, then from a kissing-gate on the right cross the field to another. A larger field is crossed towards trees on the right, from where continue along the fieldside: Stonyhurst makes a fine prospect rising across the fields. From the kissing-gate at the end, two short fieldsides lead past a meagre pond to a kissing-gate back onto the B6243. Turn right on the footway to return to the bridge.

Ribble and Hodder confluence

18 HODDER BRIDGES

4 miles from Higher Hodder Bridge

Three fine bridges span the delectable River Hodder

Start Higher Hodder Bridge (SD 697410; BB7 3LP), parking at Clitheroe end
Map OS Explorer OL41, Forest of Bowland & Ribblesdale

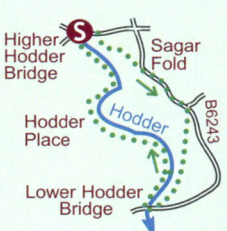

Begin by heading back up the road to Hodder Court, until 1994 the Hodder Bridge Hotel. Turn right on a drive to houses at Hodder View - ahead is Pendle Hill. Keep on a cart track to a stile at the end, sending an enclosed path off alongside a streamlet. Surrounded by delectable greenery high above a wooded curve of the unseen river, at the bottom is a stile accessing a twin-slab stone footbridge into trees. Up the other side a sunken way curves away left, and over a simple footbridge a stile transfers you into a field. Rise by the tree-lined streamlet to a stile onto a road at Sagar Fold. Longridge Fell's conifered slopes rise behind you.

Turn right for a half-mile of decent verge walking as far as a junction with the B6243. Advance just 50 yards further to a stile by a gate on the right into a vast field. Head diagonally away past two adjacent oaks, bearing left of four further neighbouring oaks to a stile/gate in a fence. Head away, merging with a fence above the steep, wooded bank of the River Hodder. Continue on to a corner stile, where a path runs through a belt of trees extending up from the bank. Over a stile at the end resume as before, ultimately dropping to a stile back onto the B6243. Turn right the very short way to Lower Hodder Bridge. Immediately downstream is the remarkable 16th century Cromwell's Bridge, so named as the historical figure came this way prior to the Battle of Preston in 1648: a little path on the other side gives access.

Across the bridge a firm track heads upstream around a big sweep of the Hodder. When the track is finally replaced by a path at a gate, this runs on to another to rise briefly steeply beneath a massive wall to approach Hodder Place. Once a junior school for Stonyhurst College, it is now residential. On the brow keep straight on a broad path down into trees. Immediately after a substantial stone bridge on a sidestream is a divergence of paths: your way tackles the flight of steps climbing to a crossroads of paths. Here go right to reach, within 50 yards, a sizeable stone cross at a lovely spot high above another great sweep of the Hodder.

Beyond it the path drops a little then runs grandly on above the river, contouring through a carpet of springtime wild garlic. It soon slants down to approach the water's edge, and well-placed footbridges on sidestreams ease the way as the path emerges onto an open bank. Delightful walking leads round further bends, with grassy banks offering the finest section of the walk. On re-entering woodland the last leg is a well-constructed path through trees, with Higher Hodder Bridge appearing ahead. At least three sets of what appear like stepping-stones are in fact salmon pools, the Hodder being a renowned fishing river. Via more footbridges the path passes right of a house before a footbridge and then steps up onto the road at the bridge.

Cromwell's Bridge

19   LONGRIDGE FELL

3¾ miles from Jeffrey Hill

Easy moorland walking with majestic views to Bowland

Start Cardwell House
(SD 639401; PR3 2TU),
car park north of road summit
Map OS Explorer OL41, Forest of Bowland & Ribblesdale
Access Open Access, concession paths

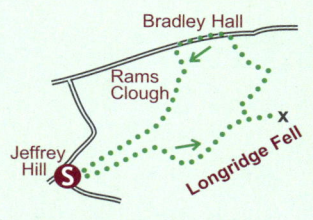

Before even pulling your boots on, savour big views across Chipping's fertile vale to the Bowland fells. From a kissing-gate at the top of the parking area, a broad path rises gently away through reedy pasture. At a stone waymark fork left to commence a level stride, passing another post to run grandly on above a steeper heathery drop to reach a streamlet. Across, the intermittently moist path rises right alongside a reedy tract, easing out to run to a wall at a plantation corner. Don't pass through but ascend the heathery, again part moist wallside, crossing a fence-stile where the Ordnance Survey column is revealed a quarter-mile ahead. Before it however a cross-path is met alongside a kissing-gate: to this you will return after the short detour to the summit, straight ahead.

The OS column at 1148ft/350m crowns the most southerly named 'fell' in England. The magnificent panorama is enhanced by the proximity of the Bowland massif: from Beacon Fell round to Waddington Fell, the heights of Parlick, Fair Snape and Totridge front this upland dome. Its foreground complements it, with the wooded Hodder gliding through green fields liberally scattered with farms. Chipping is evident towards the foot of Parlick, while further back are Ingleborough and Penyghent in the Yorkshire Dales.

Retracing steps to the path crossroads, turn right on a path rapidly gaining an edge to earn an appreciation of the fell's great northern slopes. The path swings right to enjoy a grand slant down with an old sunken way. Leaving the heather towards the bottom, double back left with the reedy way to a gate in the wall below. Bear slightly left down a large pasture to a fence-stile left of a gate. Drop down a reedy patch tapering to a messy corner at the bottom. Over a stile escape along a broadly enclosed way, where stiles and gates lead out via sheep pens onto a road at Bradley Hall.

Turn left for a short half-mile to the first drive on the left, rising to Rams Clough. Pass between the houses to a gate, and from a gate behind ascend an unkempt pasture on a grassy quad track. At a tree-lined, reedy ditch, it bears right and falters amid less endearing reedy terrain. At a junction of ditches just past a further small clump, escape reeds to rise to a final pair of trees. Now bear right beneath a pronounced bank to a forlorn gatepost, just past which swing left in front of a streamlet to a gate back onto the fell.

A little path sets off right along the base, immediately dropping briefly through dense bracken to stride the stream by the fence. Rising away the wall takes over again, bracken is escaped and the intermittently moist trod gently rises, never far above the wall. Moist reedy sections are encountered, but the way largely improves. Above a house the wall drops away: keep straight on to a sunken way just ahead. Ignoring a left branch, your path crosses this and a parallel one just beyond. The path then rises gently to fade above a reedy hollow: rise left, and with the wall just ahead a trod crosses to leave the fell where you began.

On Longridge Fell

20 RIVER BROCK

4¾ miles from Beacon Fell

The wooded banks of the Brock offer a fine ramble from a colourful miniature fell

Start *Bowland Visitor Centre (SD 564427; PR3 2EW), car park*
Map *OS Explorer OL41, Forest of Bowland & Ribblesdale*

Beacon Fell's isolated dome boasts moorland and woodland, and its visitor centre has information, shop, café and WC. With your back to the centre turn right along the road for a few minutes through the trees. At a sharp bend right, a short path goes left to a bridle-gate into a small memorial wood giving sweeping views over the Fylde. At the bottom, descend a large pasture to a kissing-gate into trees, and a path drops to a tiny footbridge into a field. Bear slightly left to a stile onto Bleasdale Road, right a few yards then down leafy White Lee Lane. This drops into woodland to ultimately reach the River Brock at Higher Brock Bridge. Don't cross but turn upstream on a driveway below a house, Brock Mill. A gate after a cottage puts you into a field which is crossed to cut a bend of the river, rejoining it before a corner stile. Enclosed by a fence the path hugs its bank through a lovely stretch, until approaching a marshy area where it turns to climb steps up the bank. Rising to meet a rough access road, go left to drop to an isolated house. To its right a path runs along the foot of a wooded bank, before the wooded river gives a short stroll to Snape Rake footbridge.

Without crossing, double back right up the steep and stony hollowed way to follow a dead-end road away. At the end of the wood on the left, enter it on a hollowed bridleway that slants back down. As it doubles sharply back left keep straight on, over a footbridge into a field. Cross this to meet a track descending from Waddecar scout centre. Advance along this, through various activity areas close by the river, and narrowing to a path to a stile out of the site. A faint path continues through a couple of fields to a footbridge spanning the southernmost of the Brock streams at their confluence, a lovely spot. Don't cross but turn right past a low ruin to a stile, and a path continues upstream through trees. Quickly finding yourself on a feeder stream, the path runs to a footbridge on it. Across, it slants right up to a stile into the open. A broad way heads directly away, bearing slightly left with the cone of Parlick as a guide, and the Bleasdale fells arrayed to its left.

Through a gate/stile ahead, follow the fence on your left to the end. Through a couple of stiles by gates, turn right with a fence through two fields to reach an enclosed path: this runs left outside the grounds of Wickens Barn onto a road. Turn right for a few minutes, and leave by a drive rising to houses. Just short of the top take a stile on the right, through a moist corner and within a minute turning sharp left at a waymark. A grassy path ascends the pasture to a stile at the top, then up open ground onto Beacon Fell Road. Virtually opposite, a broad, firm track slants right through trees. Emerging at a broad cross-paths near the wood edge, turn left 150 yards then take a firm path rising right onto open moor. This climbs rapidly to the OS column crowning Beacon Fell at 872ft/266m, a popular viewpoint. To finish follow the main path into trees ahead, dropping gently right at an immediate cross-paths, and bearing right at a junction at the bottom.

River Brock

21 PARLICK

3 miles from Fell Foot

An excellent mini fellwalk on a very popular landmark hill

Start *Fell Foot (SD 601442; PR3 3NZ), parking at and above road junction beneath Fell Foot cul-de-sac, 1½ miles north-west of Chipping*
Map *OS Explorer OL41, Forest of Bowland & Ribblesdale*
Access *Open Access/concession path, see page 4*

A favourite venue of paragliders, Parlick's neat cone dominates its surroundings on your approach to the start. From the junction rise a few strides up the lane to a stile on the left, then slant gently away across roughish pasture to a ladder-stile in the far wall. Head away to quickly join a fence on the left, a short-lived grassy track leading along to a gate. Head away to a fence-stile at a crumbling wall, then rise slightly to cross to a craftsman-built wall-stile. Now contour across a longer pasture to cross a deep streamlet just short of a corner stile behind another streamlet beneath open fellside.

Across, advance a short way to a kissing-gate in the adjacent fence and cross a plank bridge on a drain. A thin path runs left along the base of the fell to an intervening gate at a reedy corner. A better path continues, rising slightly to a gentle brow looking down on the farm at Blindhurst. This reveals a super prospect of Bleasdale's fields, farms and fells, with island-like Beacon Fell beyond. Here, above a gate, double back right up an initially faint grass track ascending from the farm. This rapidly becomes sunken and winds up the pasture to a kissing-gate back onto open fell.

The old track commences a sustained zigzag up Parlick's western flank: though often reed-filled it is dry underfoot, with a path of sorts either within or alongside. Start by going a few strides left to the old gate, then a rough path bears away right. Within fifty yards, the sunken way swings sharply back right, then quickly left

46

for a longer spell. The fell's upper slopes appear before you double back right. Further, it doubles back left to quickly arrive above a broad, reedy gully. Just fifty yards further the way turns steeply and directly up to the right. When it swings more gently left again, keep just above it on a short slant to an old wall at a lone gatepost.

Here a clear path is joined and followed left for a superb, largely level stroll across the fellside, with fine views over the bowl of Bleasdale to Fair Snape Fell. Largely contouring for some time, you suddenly arrive above a pronounced little drop to a nick in the ridge connecting with the massive bulk of Fair Snape. Here take a thin path doubling sharply back right the short way up to a kissing-gate in the ridge fence. Grassy paths rise gently up either side of it to Parlick's 1417ft/432m summit mound, with a stone shelter, the scattered stones of a former cairn, and a kissing-gate in the fence. The panorama includes Longridge Fell, Pendle Hill, Waddington Fell and round via Saddle Fell to the Bleasdale moors.

Leave by a grassy path shadowing the fence down steeper ground to soon arrive at a cross-path and kissing-gate in it. Go left to quickly meet a sunken way, which slants down across the fellside for a lengthy spell to ultimately arrive above the lone house at Fell Foot. The path finishes with a short zigzag by a modern stone shelter to reach a gate off the fell alongside the solitary house. Conclude down this short lane back to the junction.

Parlick from Beacon Fell

22   CHIPPING LANDSCAPES

3¾ miles from Chipping

Easy walking with big views from gentle slopes above a fine Bowland village

Start *Village centre (SD 632432; PR3 2GD), car park*
Map *OS Explorer OL41, Forest of Bowland & Ribblesdale*

Chipping is an attractive, tightly-packed village with pubs, cafe, Post office/shop and farm shop. St Bartholomew's church has 16th century origins and great semi-circular approach steps, while a former school endowed by cloth merchant John Brabin in 1683 stands with adjacent almshouses. Leave by the side road of Church Raikes past the church, and at a junction at the village edge fork right down to a hollow at historic Kirk Mill. Across the bridge rise past it to a large millpond. Part way along turn off at a stile by a drive, and a path slants up across a field to a fence opposite. Rising away, it levels out to run to the far end. To the left Parlick thrusts itself forward from the moorland skyline, while Longridge Fell forms a long skyline over to the right.

From the stile a faint path advances over a large field, bearing left to the bank above Dobson's Brook. Ignoring a first little path slanting left with a groove, pass beneath a small hollow, and another such path heads off above a trio of trees to contour across the rougher bank to a kissing-gate. From it the path runs on into scattered trees, crossing a footbridge on the right arm of a confluence. The path heads away then swings right to climb to the house at Windy Hills. From a gate to its left, cross the yard to one at the far side of a barn conversion, then rise to a bridle-gate from where a sunken green path climbs the fieldside.

Through a stile/gate at the top, bear right with the fence to rise gently to another. Entering dense but dry reeds, a wall takes over before another stile/gate just ahead. Forge on through reeds, and just before a brow, turn unconvincingly left across the reeds to a fence-stile behind a plank footbridge. Bear right to a corner stile onto the head of a surfaced road, and ignoring the farm road continuing uphill, turn sharp right on a track through a gate. On the brow this reveals views out to Pendle Hill and Longridge Fell, while Burnslack and Fair Oak Fells still form a great wall above you. The track enters rough pasture at a gate, and shadows a fence on your left to drop to a gate in front of Leagram Brook.

Across the ford/stepping-stones, make brief use of the access land of Stanley and bear right up the steep little bank. A trod forms to trace the rim of the brook downstream through this rough pasture, quickly reaching a bridle-gate on the right at the end. A grassy way drops down to a ford, though easiest option is a stile to the left to join the driveway of Park Gate. Turn right over a cattle-grid and bridge and away through fields to a junction with another drive. Go left to skirt the farm at Chipping Lawn and continue gently down through the pleasant parkland of Leagram Hall, with Longridge Fell a fine backdrop. Absorbing its drive, this continues down to the road. Here a concession bridleway runs right through a belt of trees, shadowing the road until joining it by a lodge. Turn right to quickly re-enter the village alongside the war memorial.

Chipping church

23   AROUND WHITEWELL

3¾ miles from Whitewell

Outstanding Hodder Valley views dominate a ramble through fields above the Whitewell Gorge

Start Hamlet centre (SD 658468; BB7 3AT), roadside parking
Map OS Explorer OL41, Forest of Bowland & Ribblesdale

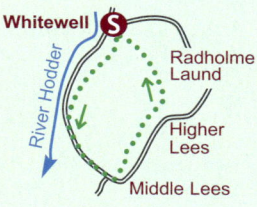

Cheek by jowl at Whitewell are pub and church - indeed not a great deal else, but it's a charming spot. The little church of St Michael dates from 1818, while the Inn at Whitewell is an old fashioned country hotel. Leave by the minor road climbing from the green bound for Clitheroe, past the social hall. Just beyond a drive turn up steps to a small gate, from which a faint path rises to a house at Seed Hill. Turn right in front of it, and a grassy track passes right of an aqueduct installation and heads across the field, slanting up past a small old quarry to the field corner. Big views look across to Totridge and up-dale to the Dunsop Valley fells.

From the gate at the top, turn right along the wallside to tall iron gates, then head away with a fence. This stage offers splendid views over the wooded Whitewell Gorge to limestone knolls beneath the moorland wall of Fair Oak Fell. When the fence slants uphill, instead bear right to a stile in a fence ahead. Resuming, you are rejoined by the upper fence to run to a gate in a wall. Continue as before with a fence, passing a small quarry with tilted rocks to reach more iron gates. Now bear gently right across an open field to a gate at the far corner, just past which is a tall gate onto the adjacent road. Follow this left, and with Longridge Fell's long, flat skyline ahead, the road gently declines to a junction at Middle Lees, with old guidestones in the base of the walls.

Go briefly left to a stile at the end of the trees, and head away to cross a sturdy footbridge. Turn upstream, passing through a stile to close in on the stream rising towards Higher Lees Farm. As the fence cuts the corner towards the top, take a stile into the stream's environs and cross towards its bank. Turn upstream to pass through a few trees, and very shortly slant back up from the bank to rise to a stile into the farm. Go briefly right on its drive, and as it swings away right, go straight on the front of the house. Through a gate continue along an enclosed track. When this leaves the greenery and turns left, go straight across the field to a stile/gate ahead. Now bear gently left up a large sloping pasture to find a stile in a wall corner alongside Park Gate Wood. Advance with the wall enclosing it, at the end revealing Radholme Laund just ahead.

Remain with the wall as it swings right with the wood, soon deflected left by a wall towards the farm. Cross at a gate part way on, resuming on the other side to a gate into the yard. Rise straight up past the house and between large barns, and continue straight up a field with a wall on your right. Reaching a brow, drop to an iron gate, then cross to one to the right. Resume with a wall on your left up to another gentle brow, and start to descend: ahead is a stunning Hodder Valley prospect looking to an array of rolling moors. This grand finish descends through a stile/gate, and towards the bottom bear right to a ladder-stile in the wall below. A thin path winds more steeply down to the house at the start, re-tracing steps down to the road on the hamlet edge.

The Inn at Whitewell

24 LITTLE BOWLAND

4¼ miles from Whitewell

Easy rambling linking old Bowland farmsteads with stunning views from limestone knolls above the Whitewell Gorge

Start Hamlet centre (SD 658468; BB7 3AT), roadside parking
Map OS Explorer OL41, Forest of Bowland & Ribblesdale

For a note on Whitewell see page 50. Leave by dropping into the hotel car park by the church, then right on its lower section where a firm path runs left to the River Hodder. This quickly leads to 56 sturdy stepping-stones taking you across in exhilarating style. If impassable, start at Burholme Bridge a mile north, and walk up the road to join the route. A path heads directly away to climb outside a wood to New Laund Farm. Advance between buildings and follow the drive as far as an old cheese press on a bend. Here a gate in front sends a green way away with a fence on the flank of New Laund Hill. Further, it swings left gently uphill, and through a gate continues rising with the fence on your left. Lovely views look back up the valley to the fells above Dunsop Bridge.

Through a gate at the top rise to a limestone knoll in front, and just before an old quarry bear right the short way to a gate onto a road. Go briefly left to a stile on the right. Over a streamlet rise left up the bank, and gently ascend the field centre to an access road just left of Tunstall Ing. Turn right past the house and along the road, with big views up-dale to distant Penyghent. The road swings left between limestone knolls to a fork, where drop left to Higher Fence Wood. Entering the farmyard, go left of the house and back out on a track dropping to Dinkling Green Brook. Across the footbridge drop left between brook and fence, lower down taking a stile in the fence. Cross to a gate just ahead, then descend a field to Dinkling Green. A small gate right of a modern barn puts you into the farmyard. Turn left on the drive out, becoming surfaced beneath Long Knots to ultimately emerge at a crossroads.

Advance straight on only as far as Higher Greystoneley drive on the right, just past which take a stile on the left. From another just behind, bear right to the many barns at Fair Oak. Pass round to the rear of the large stone barn on the left: known as the Gunnary, it has a 1729 datestone. Advance through the yard to the centre, and turn left past the house. Before the next house turn right through a gate and down a rough track, noting the house's 1716 inscribed tablet. The track drops to a gate and then runs on a fenceside away. Through a gate ahead it becomes enclosed, then drops sharp right through a stile/gate at the end to emerge into a field corner, with New Laund Hill ahead and the Whitewell Gorge down to the right. Now follow the curving fence left, rising very gently to a ladder-stile in the wall ahead.

A faint path heads away, rising gently and delightfully onto a limestone shoulder of New Laund Hill. The path briefly fades to reveal a super prospect up-dale, while behind you the gorge ushers the river through rich woodland. The path quickly re-forms to drop to a long-abandoned gateway/stile, and a faint grassy way angles gently right towards the wood edge. Descend to reveal New Laund just below, dropping more steeply through slight outcrops to a gate opposite the house. Turn right to conclude as you began.

Hodder Valley at New Laund Farm

25 HODDER BANK FELL

4¼ miles from Dunsop Bridge

A low fell with excellent views sandwiched between the banks of the delightful Hodder

Start Village centre (SD 660500; BB7 3BB), car park
Map OS Explorer OL41, Forest of Bowland & Ribblesdale

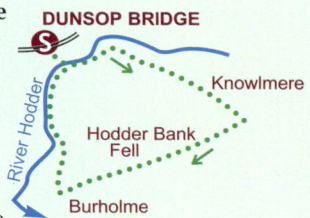

Dunsop Bridge claims to mark the centre of Great Britain and 401 associated islands - see the phone box. By the riverside green are St George's church, Post office/shop/tearoom and WC. Leave the eastern end of the village past the car park, then take a drive on the right to bridge the Hodder at Thorneyholme Hall. Immediately across, take a small gate on the left from where a path squeezes tightly between riverbank and wall. At the wall end emerge and take a small gate on the right into a field. Bear left, diverging steadily away from the river to an outer fence corner, then along to a stile ahead, with a tree-lined stream behind. Now bear right up to meet a wall at an old boundary. Through a stile in the wall, turn left on a grassy concession path which makes for a grand stride along to a gate. As a clearer track it advances across open pasture, rising slightly to run through lovely surroundings to a gate alongside a house at Mossthwaite.

Pass through and out on the drive past another house. This runs on for some time, becoming surfaced to pass Victorian Knowlmere Manor amid pleasant parkland. A nice encounter with the Hodder precedes arrival at Giddy Bridge on Birkett Brook. Don't cross, but double back right up a grassy bank to a stile/gate in a wall above, then up to a fence-stile. Rising away, slant gently right up to a fence-stile at a distinct ditch part way up, well short of the barn at Matril Laithe. Now rise directly away to a bridle-gate that appears in the skyline wall above, between small plantations.

This accesses the open spaces of Hodder Bank Fell, and a path rises through grassy moorland tussocks. Quickly gaining the brow, a stone post marks the walk's high point at about 656ft/200m.

Occasionally moist, the path encounters further stone posts as it runs grandly on before dropping gently to a corner of the fell. From the ladder-stile a fine path escapes a moist patch and heads away, enjoy a sustained descent through bracken by a fence on the edge of Fielding Clough. Big views look over the valley to a long moorland skyline dominated by Totridge. At the bottom, with the farm at Burholme just below, a kissing-gate finally crosses the fence. Drop down the field to a stile just above the stream, then down a little further to a footbridge by the farm.

Don't use it but take the grassy track emerging from the farm to head right across two pleasant pastures (gates/stiles) to close in on the Hodder. A rough pasture is entered via an old iron gate/stile, and a path marginally short-cuts the confluence of Langden Brook with the river. Passing an aqueduct, continue along your bank through a stile then plank bridge and small gate before an extensive tree-lined pasture leads to a farm drive at Thorneyholme. The path is ushered round the outside, past a lovely watersmeet as it absorbs the River Dunsop to reach a small gate back onto the bridge near the start.

River Hodder, Dunsop Bridge

26. NEWTON-IN-BOWLAND

3¼ miles from Newton

Riverside and fieldpaths from a charming village, with open views

Start Village centre (SD 697504; BB7 3DY), car park on edge
Map OS Explorer OL41, Forest of Bowland & Ribblesdale

Newton-in-Bowland is a lovely stone village overlooking the sparkling River Hodder. Across from the late Georgian Parkers Arms is the attractive Newton Hall, while other delightful old buildings overlook luxuriant greens. Leave by descending to Newton Bridge on the Hodder, and across it take a kissing-gate on the right. Head down-river, not quite on the bank as you pass a fence corner to find a stile at the end. The path then runs atop a grassy bank to join the river fully. After a short while, through another stile the river turns away at a wooded bank, and here bear left to a gate/stile half-way up the fence ahead. Continue slanting left to a gate and then on towards a house that appears ahead at Foulscales. In the hedge to its left is a stile onto a road.

Turn briefly right, crossing Foulscales Brook to two barns, after which go right along a surfaced access road. After a quarter mile, take a stile on the right and cross a field to another, where marshy ground leads to a suspension footbridge. Re-crossing the Hodder in exhilarating fashion, rise gently away up the field, bearing left to a fence-stile just short of Knoll Wood. Continue past a limestone quarry eaten into the knoll, and on to a footbridge on a stream. From this cross to a stile onto a road, and go right just 150 yards as far as a stile on the left. Cross the field into a wooded corner to meet a long-abandoned drive.

From a gate/stile in front, head away with a pond at the isolated house of The Heaning over the hedge to your left. At the end cross a drive to a corner stile, then ascend a sloping mire to dry ground above. Continue rising with a line of trees to a ladder-stile at the top. Head away with a distinct former field boundary onto the brow, where big views feature Totridge, Hodder Bank Fell and Easington Fell, with Beatrix Fell and Burn Fell just to your left. Advance to a wall-stile just further right, by a massive stone gatepost. Continue on the wallside ahead to a stile onto a back road. For a direct finish turn right, passing on the brow a Quaker burial ground, while lower down is the old Friends' Meeting House: dating from the 1760s, it ceased to function in 1988.

From a stile opposite, head away to drop to a footbridge on a tiny stream. Behind, pass through a narrowing into another field, bearing right on a part sunken way to a stile ahead. Head directly away through a wood, soon reaching an open edge on the right from where continue alongside the trees. Dropping gently to cross a streamlet, negotiate fallen trees to reach a gate/stile at the bottom corner. Leaving the trees ignore a stile on your left, and double sharply back right down the sloping pasture to re-cross the previous streamlet above a confluence. Maintain this line, through a gate then a gateway and along to a gate/stile at the end. Advance to a gate into a garden just ahead, passing left of the house and then left on the short driveway down into the village.

The Hodder at Newton

27 RIVER HODDER

3¾ miles from Slaidburn

A brief ascent gives wide views before an easy descent to the bank of the delectable Hodder

Start Village centre (SD 711524; BB7 3EP), car park
Map OS Explorer OL41, Forest of Bowland & Ribblesdale

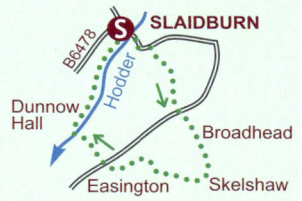

For a note on Slaidburn see page 60. Leave by crossing the bridge on the River Hodder, a splendid vantage point for the confluence with Croasdale Brook immediately upstream. Across, ignore a stile on the left and take a gate ahead into a yard. Cross to a gate at the end, and take a path slanting steeply right up to a gap-stile at the top. Drop briefly right on the road to a gate on the left, and an inviting path rises away. Big views look back over the village to the moorland wall beyond. Approaching a wall, bear left with it on a path running to a stile at the far end. Ascend the continuing wallside past a plantation: this brow reveals a fuller prospect of Easington Fell ahead. After the trees take a gate in the wall to resume on its other side, descending to a road: cross straight over on the drive down to Broadhead Farm.

Pass left of the buildings and round the back to a farm bridge on Easington Brook. Bear right across a fenced enclosure to a gate into a field, and cross to another in a fence just ahead. Slant right up the large field with Skelshaw Brook to the right. In the hidden top corner, ignore a tiny footbridge in favour of a gate on the right. Across a small stream, advance to stepping-stones on Skelshaw Brook just beyond. Rise to a bridle-gate in a fence just above, with another gate up behind. Bear left up the fieldside outside the wooded brook, curving up to a gate at the large house at Skelshaw. Turn right on the access road to commence a long, simple descent to the valley at Easington. This gives ample time to appraise an extensive panorama of the vast slopes of Totridge, Beatrix, Dunsop and Croasdale Fells beyond the Hodder Valley. At the bottom the drive bridges Easington Brook and runs briefly downstream to a fork. Branch right to the imposing Manor House, passing right of the buildings, through the farmyard and out onto a narrow road.

Go left a few strides to a gate opposite, and head directly away with a fence: this is soon crossed at an iron kissing-gate in a recess. Turn right down the field centre, aiming left of the trees to find another such gate in a dip. Beneath it is an old iron footbridge on a reedy drain, from where cross to a broad bridge on the Hodder: ahead is the Victorian mansion of Dunnow Hall. Across, ignore the track towards the hall, and turn right on a permissive path upstream in glorious surrounds. An impressive limestone scar thrusts out of the wooded bank above, while Slaidburn church soon appears ahead. A sewage works deflects the path around three sides of it, joining the access road through a gate and then over a stile to cross back to the river. Its bank is traced all the way back to the village, with just one intervening stile before later becoming enclosed to run above a wooded bank to emerge onto the green.

The Hark to Bounty, Slaidburn

28 CROASDALE

4 miles from Slaidburn

An unassuming but charming circuit of Croasdale Brook on largely delectable fieldpaths

Start Village centre (SD 711524; BB7 3EP), car park
Map OS Explorer OL41, Forest of Bowland & Ribblesdale

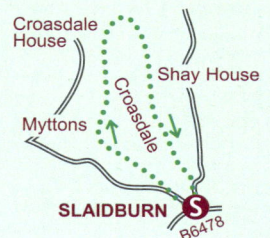

Slaidburn has been capital of Bowland since the days of the hunting forest, and the Hark to Bounty pub was home to the forest courts. St Andrew's church dates from the 15th century: adjacent is the grammar school of 1717 that survives as the village school. There is a Post office/shop, tearooms, Bowland Chocolates, youth hostel and a heritage centre, while the River Hodder flows by a spacious green. Leave by a side road along the front of the pub, and immediately after the health centre take a path into trees on the right. Trace Croasdale Brook to a stile, shortly after which the path slants left up to adjacent small gates into a field. Head away with the hedge, crossing a farm track to a stile at the end. A thin path advances on with the brook again to a wall-stile at the end. Over a stone slab bridge on a sidestream, gently ascend the field centre to a corner gate. Rise away with a wall, swinging right with it at the top on a short, enclosed green way leading to Myttons.

From a stile left of the house bear right over a field to a corner stile onto a track. Go right over the bridge to derelict Bridge End, and take a small gate to its left. Rise above the stream to a wall-stile left of a barn, then cross a long pasture to a stile at the far end. Emerging with big views to a long moorland skyline, cross the field to a gate/stile. Advance straight on over a gentle brow, then drop slightly left to a stile just right of a driveway near the far corner. A path contours right across a sloping field under the house at Simfield, to a small gate beneath it. The path leads past the garden edge to a tiny footbridge into trees, then drops right down the wooded bank to a kissing-gate at the bottom. Just ahead is a footbridge on Croasdale Brook, the walk's turning point.

Joining Croasdale House drive turn right, away from the farm and on past large, modern barns. After bridging a tree-lined stream, cross to a kissing-gate near the brook. Cross the field centre to a kissing-gate onto a drive, with Shay House Farm to the right. Don't cross the bridge to the farm, but from a stile almost opposite resume downstream. As the brook curves away, keep straight on to a ladder-stile in the wall ahead. Head away with a streamlet, and as it swings right bear left to the start of a wall, briefly overlooking a bend of the brook again. Ascend briefly with the wall to a stile in the corner above. Across a track rise away with an old field boundary, continuing up to a wall-stile on the very brow. Pause to look back on a glorious scene to the fells enclosing Croasdale.

Resume directly away across a vast field, on a slight dome with big views all round. Through an intervening stile, slowly bear left to a corner stile at the end of a line of trees. Head directly away through the few trees to reveal Slaidburn ahead: initially with a line of trees, your path descends delightfully towards it. Lower down, locate a stile onto the road before the bottom, and go right to bridge Croasdale Brook before entering the village.

The bridge and green at Slaidburn

29 TROUGH OF BOWLAND

3¾ miles from Sykes

A rough moorland tramp at the very heart of Bowland

Start Sniddle Holes (SD 626526; BB7 3BJ), parking area at foot of steep drop from road summit west of Sykes Farm, 3 miles west of Dunsop Bridge
Map OS Explorer OL41, Forest of Bowland & Ribblesdale

Access Open Access, see page 4

Turn back down the road from the pass, becoming enclosed to reach Trough Barn. Amid steep fellsides, this side valley through the Trough of Bowland was the way the Pendle Witches were transported to Lancaster Assizes. Through the gate at the barn a firm track climbs above a wooded bank, outside a plantation. Easing out it runs more pleasantly to the top end of a small wood, and through the gate/stile are the remains of Trough House. Leaving by another gate, the track rises right with a wall. Ahead is a deep bowl below the horseshoe of Whins Brow and Staple Oak Fell. Curving uphill the track passes through a gate/stile in the wall to run briefly between a small wood and a wall.

Opening into rougher terrain, a grassy way continues with the wall until it drops away. A contrastingly thin path takes over to slant all the way up to a bridle-gate in a wall. In Open Access land, a grand little path climbs the moor alongside a scarred gully to quickly gain the level moor-top. Joining a fence from the right, the path runs more moistly to a fence junction on the watershed. You shall return here after a short detour to view the Brennand Valley from above. Through the bridle-gate head on through moister, heathery terrain, quickly swinging left to find the ground suddenly falling away. The Ouster Rake path here commences an enjoyable descent, but all you need do is find a heathery couch and savour the moment. Directly below is Brennand Farm, its pastures wrapped in a moorland bowl running from Ward's Stone to Wolfhole Crag.

Back at the boundary fence, pass through and turn right up the fenceside. An intermittent trod stays close to the fence on this gentle rise encountering modest peat banks but largely reasonably dry. Eventually easing, the Ordnance Survey column on Whins Brow is revealed: if you need to touch it, then use the kissing-gate just before it and return through another just beyond the top. At 1561ft/476m, the walk's summit is a lonely spot from which to appraise a sweeping Bowland scene. While Totridge rises back across the Trough, eyes are drawn westwards to the Ward's Stone skyline with the Fylde Coast beyond. To the north are shapely Whernside, Ingleborough and Penyghent, Yorkshire's Three Peaks.

Resume with the fence dropping gently away to a fence junction. A distinct trod cuts this corner and remains distant from the fence for a while, giving a view down to a section of road at Trough Barn. Rejoining the fence, this descends gently on good, dry moor-grass. Lower down, a tussocky corner sees a fence come in from the left. Step over this to reveal, two minutes further, the summit of the Trough road below, and a steeper final minute puts you onto the road – perhaps avoiding a swamp by stepping over the wooden fence to the other side of the cattle-grid. On the crest at 968ft/295m stands the historic Grey Stone of Trough, marking the traditional Yorkshire-Lancashire boundary. Finish by turning left for a short, relatively steep drop back to the start.

Brennand Valley from Ouster Rake

30 LANGDEN VALLEY

3¾ miles from Langden Intake

An easy excursion into the recesses of a remote Bowland valley

Start Langden Intake
(SD 632511; BB7 3BH),
popular parking area on Trough road 2 miles west of Dunsop Bridge
Map OS Explorer OL41, Forest of Bowland & Ribblesdale
Access Open Access (can be avoided), see page 4

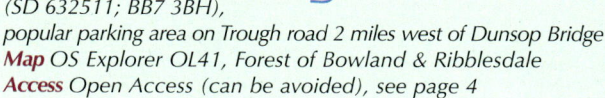

The parking area has an air crash memorial and occasional refreshments. Head away on the drive to Langden House, bearing right of it and quickly ending at the intake works. Beyond a gate a firm track sets out into the lonely valley of Langden Brook. A spell by the brook precedes a brief, steep climb above a tiny wooded bank. On levelling out it forks: keep left for easy walking on a largely level terrace, with time to become acquainted with this lovely dale. After minor undulations, a more marked rise to a junction can be eschewed at a fence corner where a little path maintains its contour through bracken: the fence returns briefly but then drops away before you rejoin the track. Langden Castle appears ahead, and the track descends the short way to a gate in front of it.

The 'castle' is merely a shooters'/shepherds' shelter: the grassy sward at the front is a good place to sit and gaze into the side valley of Bleadale. Return through the gate and stay on the track past the path entry point, soon emerging on a knoll with a colourful footpath sign and a wartime air crash memorial. Whilst you could remain on the main track, make use of Open Access and opt for the inviting, grassier track bearing left. This makes an appreciable pull across the moorland flank, a super climb with exquisite views that levels out onto the walk's high point. A branch comes down from the left and you contour round for a while before commencing a return to the valley. This still splendid track angles down to the outward junction: go left to finish as you began.